30 DAYS TO INCREASE YOUR FAITH

30 DAYS TO INCREASE YOUR FAITH

When life happens

Eugene Minnifield

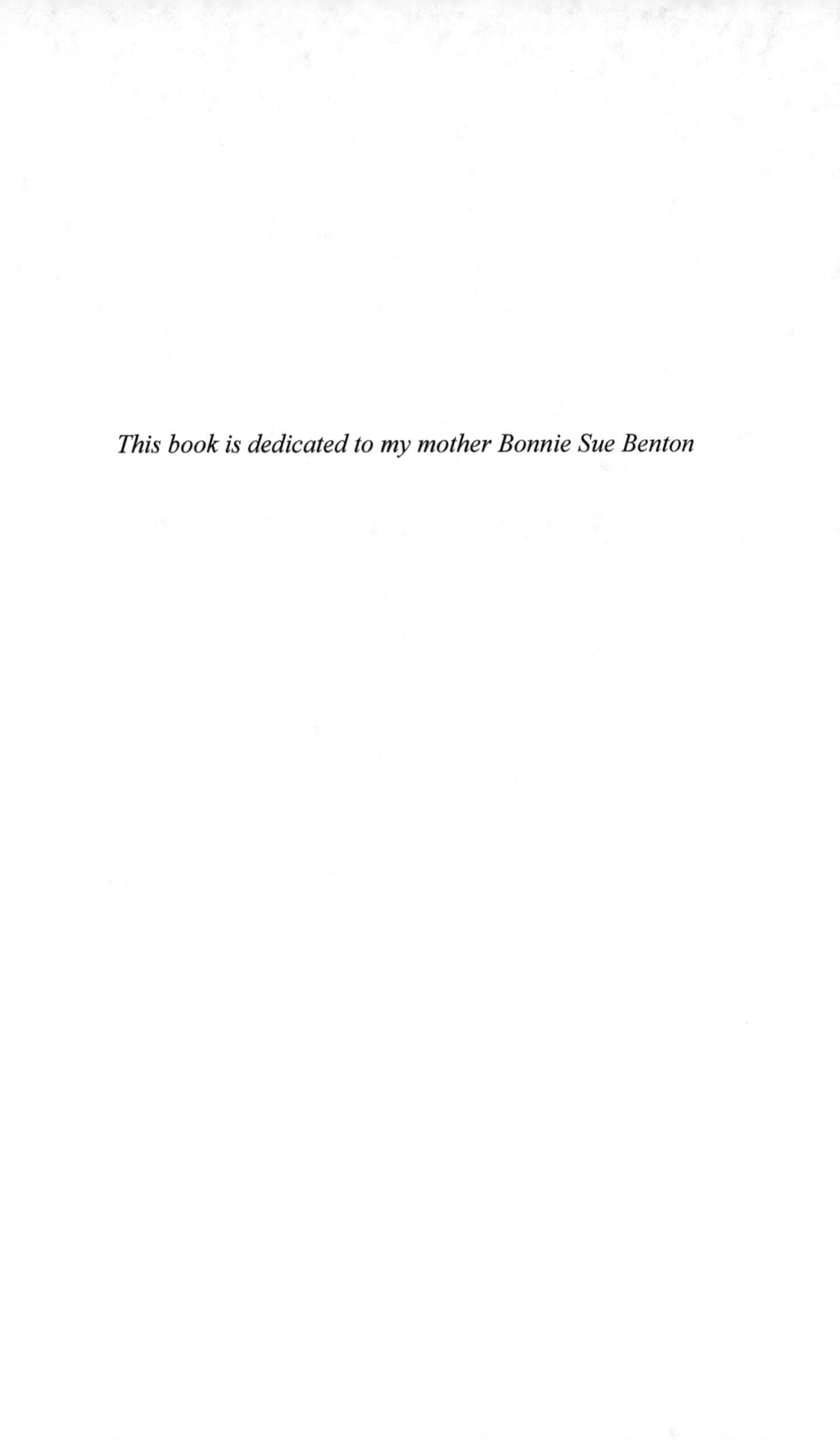

This book is dedicated to my mother Bonnie Sue Benton

Contents

Introduction

Although life has many blessings, Jesus was right when he said we would face difficulties in this world.

Numerous factors can make the road ahead appear bleak and make us feel lost and helpless in our ability to handle life.

I have two dear friends: One who just found out he has cancer and another whose wife just left.

You might probably relate to having problems and feeling that there are a lot of unknowns ahead. You appear unable to see more than a few inches before you. Not to mention which route you ought to take!

Sometimes you may feel alone and worry about how you'll make it.

The good news is that the Bible provides us with direction in the circumstances like these. No matter what challenges life presents, it teaches us that we have everything we need for a life of faith since it is brimming with wisdom and wealth.

When God called Abraham to uproot himself and his household from his home in Harran (new day Turkey), God asked him to leave behind everything he knew and live on nothing but vows.

God said he'd give him a new territory to call his own. He said he'd give Abraham a child. So many descendants. They'd be too numerous to count! He said that someday all the nations of the earth would be blessed because of Abraham's large family.

What's the issue with all of this? God wasn't letting him know where he was going on this voyage of trust. What country? Abraham had no view of any land.

And given that both Abraham and his wife were older and unable to procreate, how was Abraham supposed to have descendants?

Abraham was called to build the new nation of Israel, although he had no idea of this. A people selected by God to show the world His majesty.

Abraham was also unaware that the Lord Jesus, who would benefit all nations, would come from his family. We are aware of that. However, Abraham could not imagine how he might bear a kid.

But when God asked Abraham to leave his house and travel to a foreign land, Abraham made a significant decision.

He did what he was told.

And that was the turning point!

This means moving on in faith even when we cannot see what is ahead.

Abraham constructed altars as he traveled to a distant land to sacrifice animals and worship God.

Drawing close to God as Abraham did is one of the keys to living a life of faith. This is especially true when we are unsure of our future or what life has in store for us.

Of course, as followers of Christ, we don't construct altars or offer sacrifices, but we still need to approach him in prayer and worship to receive the assistance we so desperately need.

Therefore, let us fearlessly approach the throne of our merciful God. There we shall find grace to assist us when we are most in need and experience His mercy (Hebrews 4:16, NLT).

God, however, can appear far away when we are going through a difficult time. And maintaining spiritual practices like prayer and Bible reading can be extremely challenging.

May I recommend you lighten up on these things when times are tight rather than give up on them?

Even five minutes of straightforward prayer and reading a little Scripture section can be beneficial when we need God the greatest.

Abraham had to follow God's lead when he traveled to a new land. Often, our challenging conditions signal we need to do the same thing.

Confusion is one of the things that is quite difficult when we are facing difficult conditions with numerous unknowns.

We might need to make challenging healthcare decisions for ourselves or a loved one. Perhaps we don't know how to handle problems with our children or marriage.

God doesn't want us to fumble around in bewilderment, despite the issues and concerns we may have about our circumstances. When we ask in confidence, He promises that we have access to His wisdom for our situation.

Ask our benevolent God for wisdom, and he will grant it to you. He won't chastise you for asking. Be certain that your faith is in God alone when you ask him, though. Keep your resolve because a person with two allegiances is as unstable as a wave of the sea tossed and driven by the wind (James 1:5–6, NLT).

Throughout his travels, Abraham clung to the promises God had made to him. He believed God would provide a means for it, as He had promised to give him a kid and numerous offspring. He believed God would grant the Promised Land to him and his offspring.

Abraham led a life mostly by walking in faith, even though he occasionally doubted God and didn't always show complete trust.

The same is true for us; we must press.

I challenge you to a 30-day faith walk and a better faith life.

DAY 1-GETTING TO KNOW GOD

Bible Scripture: Proverb 8:17

I adore those who love me, and those who crave me find me. Because "God's invisible qualities—his eternal power and divine nature—have been seen, being understood from what has been formed, since the creation of the world, God has "made it obvious" that He is real. As a result, "Humans are without excuse" (Romans 1:19-20). Most attempt to increase religious knowledge, while some want to repress it. A Christian's deepest desire is to know God more (Psalm 25:4).

Therefore, we must begin with trust. Knowing God's appointed messenger, Jesus Christ, is the first step to a deeper understanding of God (John 6:38). We can start learning about God, His nature, and His will once we have been born again via the power of the Holy Spirit. "Even God's deepest things are searched for by the Spirit" (1 Corinthians 2:10). The opposite is also true: "The person without the Spirit... cannot understand [the things of God] since they are discerned only via the Spirit" (verse 14). The "natural" man and the "spiritual" man are distinct.

According to Romans 10:17, "Faith, therefore, is through earshot, and hearing by the Word of Christ." It cannot be magnified how important it is to study the Bible to get to know God better. Since we have already tasted how excellent the Lord is, we must, "Like newborn babies, want sweet, pure milk, so that by it [we] may develop in [our] salvation" (1 Peter 2:2-3). Our "delight" should be in God's Word (Psalm 119:16, 24).

People who obey the directive to be filled with the Holy Spirit are also learning more about God. The Holy Spirit is always present in born-again believers, but Ephesians 5:15–21 instructs us to walk in the Spirit and submit to His will.

Prayer:

DAY 2-BUILDING A PRAYER LIFE

Bible Scripture: Colossians 4:2

"Proceed steadfastly in prayer, being cautious in it with thanksgiving."

The majority of Christians don't consistently pray. According to research done in the past, the typical Christian participant prayed for just three minutes each day. Too many Christians only take prayer seriously at times of need.

Many people know how to pray, yet they rarely do so. Some Christians who were fervent prayer warriors in the past no longer pray.

You must develop a regular prayer life if you consider yourself a Christian. The vast majority will admit that we don't pray as we should.

. . .

Through effective prayer, the first has a significant impact on his world. The second group only prays during difficult times and typically complains about their situation rather than claiming victory through faith.

Do you regularly pray each day? Do you frequently have prayers answered? Feeling close to God?

You can!

Prayer:

DAY 3-CHOOSE A PRAYING TIME

Bible Scripture: Mark 1:35

"He left and went to a lonely area in the morning, rising well before daylight, and he prayed there."

Include prayer in your everyday routine. What is scheduled is completed.

If so, when is it better to pray? There is never a bad time to pray, without a doubt. When I was a new Christian, I prayed at night. The Lord once revealed to me that I was being beaten all day and got support from Him at night. Why not ask for His help in the morning and benefit from it all day?

I started my day with prayer and have been blessed over the years.

Pray before you begin your day. Jesus acted in that manner. He would occasionally rise early in the morning to pray. How much more should we start our days in prayer if our spotless Lord did?

. . .

Here's a helpful tip. Schedule multiple times a day to pray. Emergencies happen, and schedules get turned upside down. If you miss your primary prayer time, you will have gaps in your schedule to make it up later in the day. For example, you could plan to pray for ten minutes during your lunch break.

Prayer:

DAY 4-PICK A PRAYING PLACE

Bible Scripture: Luke 22:39-41

"He then fled and made his way to the Mount of Olives as was his tradition, followed by his disciples. When he arrived, he told them to pray to avoid falling prey to temptation. He then moved away from them by approximately the distance of a cast stone, kneeled, and prayed."

Ensuring you don't slip away from God amid life's busyness requires setting aside time and space for prayer.

Jesus cherished visiting the Olivet Mount.

Jesus had a preferred location for prayer. You, too, ought to have a space to worship.

Choose a calm, comfortable area of your home. Pray there frequently.

You might choose an outdoor location to pray as well. Maybe a certain location or a path you take when walking and praying.

When you travel, it's simple to lose your spiritual rhythm. Finding a new location to pray while you are gone, you can stay devoted to prayer even when you are not in your usual pattern. For instance, after setting my bags down in a hotel room, I choose where I want to pray.

Pick a location. Own it. Use it every day.

Prayer:

DAY 5-KEEP A RECORD OF PRAYER

Bible Scripture: Philippians 4:13
I can do all everything through Christ, who strengthens me.

Keep a prayer journal to help you stay consistent. It keeps track of your routines so you can be inspired or correct yourself when you falter.

People who enjoy writing or become easily sidetracked while praying can benefit greatly from this form of prayer journaling. It may make evident what you most desire God to know about you and what you need from Him. Instead of mentally speaking with God, writing down your prayer can help make your desires more obvious. You may even try having God write you a letter. When you use this style of prayer journaling, you could be shocked by what God speaks to you. People who enjoy writing or become easily sidetracked while praying can benefit greatly from this form of prayer journaling. It may make evident what you most desire God to know about you and what you need from Him. Instead of mentally speaking with God, writing down your prayer can help make your desires more obvious. You may even try having God write you a letter. This type of prayer journaling may surprise you with what God has to say.

A good record has four components:

- When you pray, the date.
- How long do you spend in prayer?
- Prayers are answered as a result.
- How many consecutive days have you prayed?

Write about how God works in your heart in this space.

Decide to keep a record of your prayer practices. You can either purchase a prayer journal or make one on a plain piece of paper. A spreadsheet or document can be used to build one, and then your devices can sync it.

Prayer:

DAY 6-REFLECTING ON GOD'S PROMISES

Bible Scripture: Exodus 14:14

"The Lord will compete for you, and you have only to be silent."

In life, challenging situations frequently appear out of nowhere, dropping directly onto our path. You are currently only able to see a mountain. It obstructs your advancement and your ability to see what lies ahead. We lose faith in God when we concentrate on the mountain.

The Bible records instances of God's people overcoming challenges with His assistance. Ask God to give you the strength to push past your obstacle or up your mountain. Your trust will soon overshadow all your mountains as God takes you by the hand and guides you to triumph.

                    Eugene Minnifield

Prayer:

DAY 7-TRUST GOD'S PLAN

Bible Scripture: Proverb 16:9

"The heart of man plots his way, but the Lord solidifies his steps."

When we encounter a challenging situation or receive unpleasant news, it frequently rocks us to the core and causes us fear. Consistently placing your faith in God's purposes is the best approach to developing the kind of faith that never wavers. He has plans to make your future prosperous since he knows it. Even if our journey is paved with tears, God is not surprised by life-altering events.

Keep Jeremiah 29:11 in your memory and your heart. This line from the Bible might remind you that you are never alone when tempted to question God's involvement in your life. Walking with Him is the only approach to developing complete trust in the Lord.

We can live by faith, knowing that God's will for us is "Good, pleasing, and perfect" if we acknowledge that He is trustworthy, that He has a plan for our lives, and that His plans are better than anything we could ever ask or conceive (Rom. 12:2).

Do you have faith in Him? We urge you to read God's Word and meditate on it. Living a life devoted to the trustworthy one begins with trusting His plan.

Prayer:

DAY 8-READ AND MEMORIZE GOD'S WORD

Bible Scripture: Psalms 119:105

"Thy word is a lamp unto my foundations and a light unto my path."

Our hearts and minds are filled with many negative thoughts, most of which are useless during difficult times. In contrast, the Bible is a pillar of fire that illuminates the darkness of adversity for us.

The Bible makes God's goodness and constancy clear. Knowing more about the God you worship will help you have a stronger faith. Bible verse memorization will be of assistance to you in trying times. After going through your ordeal, you will succeed. You won't prevail because of your strength but rather because you put your faith in God. Your trust will grow as you triumph each time with the aid of God's Word. Our hearts and minds are filled with many negative thoughts, most of which are useless during difficult moments. In contrast, the Bible is a pillar of fire that illuminates the darkness of adversity for us.

The Bible makes God's goodness and constancy clear. Knowing more about the God you worship will help you have a stronger faith. When facing difficulties, having Bible Scriptures in memory will be beneficial. After going through your ordeal, you will succeed. You won't prevail because of your strength but rather because you put your faith in God. Your trust will grow as you triumph each time with the aid of God's Word.

PRAYER:

DAY 9-GUARD YOUR BOND WITH GOD

Bible Scripture: Luke 10:27

"Love the Lord your God with your soul, spirit, courage, and sanity; and love your neighbor as yourself."

One thing the Bible says about prayer is that to have a genuinely effective prayer life and we must protect our hearts against anything that can hinder our relationship with God. After all, James 5:16 asserts that a righteous person's prayer has enormous strength. God answers the prayers of the righteous, according to Proverbs 15:8–29, Psalm 34:15, and 1 Peter 3:12.

The Bible is equally clear that righteousness facilitates prayer, though. As Psalm 66:18 (NIV) and Proverbs 28:9 both affirm, "One who shuts away his ear from hearing the constitution, even his prayer is an abomination" and "If I had admired guilt in my soul, the Lord would not have heard," respectively. First, Peter 3:7 also clarifies that how husbands treat their spouses affects the efficacy of their prayers.

 Eugene Minnifield

PRAYER:

DAY 10-TAKE YOUR THOUGHT CAPTIVE

Bible Scripture: 1 Thessalonians 2:13

"And we also thank God frequently because, when you obtained the word of God, which you heard from us, you earned it not as a human word, but as it is, the word of God, which is kindly at work in you who believe."

Many Christians have doubts, and the Bible tells us that we are not the only people. Even Thomas could not recognize Christ when he saw Him, and John had doubts about the identity of the Savior.

God never stops calling His children out into deeper waters and uncharted territory6. Why? To teach us to put our faith in Him. So how do you respond to unbelieving doubt? Ask the Lord's pardon in prayer and confession. Utilize God's Word to combat your doubt. Look up Bible scriptures that will encourage you to submit every thought to Christ and make them captive. You'll be surprised at how much your trust will increase if you ask the Lord to give you the faith to go through your doubt.

. . .

Prayer:

DAY 11-REJECT ANY FAITH SUBSTITUTION

Bible Scripture: Micah 7:7-8

"But I wait for God, my Savior, and I watch in faith that the one would hear me. My enemy, do not gloat over me! Despite my fall, I will get back up. The LORD will be my light even though I sit in the dark."

The Old Testament describes how some of God's people relied on things other than Him. The outcomes were terrible and heartbreaking. We can trust many idols in today's culture, but they are worthless to the Living God.

Even good things like work, family, and the church can become idols, and God vehemently condemns all forms of idolatry. Ask Him in prayer to show you if you have placed something other than Him at the center of your Holy Spirit.

To help you dismantle any alternatives, He discloses and to strengthen your faith in God alone. You will have more faith after the Lord assists you in removing the impediments to progress.

. . .

Prayer:

DAY 12-ALIGNING YOUR LIFE WITH GOD

Bible Scripture: AMOS 3:3

"How can two be together unless they agree."

Sin weakens our belief in God and makes us feel like we no longer have God's love. Incline toward Adam and Eve in the Garden of Eden, and we escape God's presence when we don't feel loved or ashamed. We are driven by faith in God and His Word by our emotions.

Repentance and sin-confession are two excellent ways to strengthen your faith. Admitting God's purity and aligning your plans under His domination will open your life up to new and sensational ways to grow your faith. If you have a sin that needs to be forgiven, ask God to reveal it to you. You honor God and begin your path to deeper faith as you make doing, His will help your heart's desire.

Sin causes everything to become out of balance. We will not be guided by the Holy Spirit acting through our spirits because our spirits will not be tuned into God. We will follow the flesh and the carnal intellect instead. The misalignment increases as a result. And that makes our lives more painful. Our souls think and act incorrectly when the spirit man is not in charge, and our bodies succumb to the world, the flesh, and the devil. The more we go our own way, the more we stray from God's intended course.

We require a correction from the Lord to bring us back into harmony with his will, just like a body that becomes out of alignment and requires a chiropractic adjustment.

Prayer:

DAY 13-PUT OTHERS' NEEDS FIRST

Bible Scripture: MATTHEW 22:37

"And he said to him, "You shall adore the Lord your God with all your spirit, heart, and mind.""

Often, we see people who seem to illuminate courage and faith in God. If we are credible, we wish we had that kind of faith. How did they get to their spiritual situation? They walked out of the boat, tested the waters, and believed God would hold them up or educate them to paddle.

Serving others is an excellent direction to step out in faith and see how God helps. The first aspect is to find something you appreciate doing and serve in that area. Your church should have many chances to serve. If they do not have a church for you, then start one! God can utilize your joy to catalyze growth in your life and impact the lasting life of others.

For God to be exalted, we are asked to be humble and lower ourselves. One excellent method to achieve this is to serve others. People notice when we go above and beyond to assist them. It is becoming less common for people to watch out for others in a society that values individual and personal achievement.

Small, everyday gestures like bringing someone coffee in the morning or sending a pal a thoughtful note can show how we care about others. The act itself need not be significant; what counts is putting others before oneself. Being thoughtful of others is another way to view this.

Develop your thinking and character.

Prayer:

DAY 14-DISCOVER WHAT WORKS FOR YOU

Bible Scripture: Jeremiah 29:11

"For I know the agendas I have for you proclaims the Lord, plans to flourish you and not to harm you, schemes to give you wish and a future."

God designed us as distinct individuals called to certain circumstances so that each person will have a distinctive approach to practicing disciplines like fasting, planned prayer, and group prayer.

You may, for instance, journal about your day in a way that is aimed toward God or writes your scheduled prayers in a journal. Another option is to utilize a list of written prayers or prayer requests to organize your prayer times. You might put these supplications in a notebook and carry them wherever you go or post them where you like to pray.

Perhaps you've found that your scheduled prayers are most effective in the mornings when you can pray for the day ahead and ask God to direct your words and deeds. You could find that you can pray more effectively while strolling outside, kneeling in a "Prayer closet," or curled up in your favorite recliner. Another option is to put passages and prayer points where you'll see them all day to encourage spontaneous prayer.

Whatever the details, find what works for you and take pleasure in the increased closeness to God that emerges.

The future?

He might completely alter your life.

Prayer:

DAY 15-USE YOUR SHIELD OF FAITH

Bible Scripture:2 Corinthians 5:7

"For we step by faith, not by sight."

Spiritual conflict is one of our faith's greatest enemies. Although the book of Ephesians was written by the apostle Paul in 60 AD, God's Word is still relevant and active today.

Satan wants God's children to question and lose faith. Satan tries to weaken our faith because it serves as a defense against his fiery darts (Ephesians 6:16). Read Ephesians 6 and incorporate the Armor of God into your daily life before you notice your faith waning. Verse 10 tells us to "Be strong in the Lord and the ability of His might," which is the key to having enough trust. We are powerless to do anything, but our confidence in God releases His power. Confessionally ask for His strength and protection in prayer. Ask Him to increase your faith so you can withstand anything the enemy throws.

Prayer:

DAY 16-GET RID OF PROUD THINKING

Bible Scripture: Psalms 139:23-24

"Search me, God, and know my heart;

test me and know my worried thoughts.

See if there is any horrible way in me."

Our faith suffers greatly due to pride, which undermines our confidence in God. Because of the illusion that pride teaches us we already know the answers, we place more value on our knowledge than on God's truth. We might use Psalm 139:23–24 as a guide to examine our life for any offensive behaviors.

Ask the Father in prayer to show you any areas of your life where pride has taken over, and then ask Him to forgive you. Note everything He reveals in a journal, then look for Bible verses to assist you in conquering these arrogant tendencies. You will become more confident in God's promises as you pray and make an effort to put pride in your life. A greater faith in His

love for us and a closer relationship result from the increased
trust.

Prayer:

DAY 17-PRACTICE CONTENTMENT

Bible Scripture:1 Timothy 6:6-7

"But godliness with contentment is a great profit.

We brought nothing into the nation and can take nothing out of it."

I t isn't easy to be content when things do not turn out as we had hoped or when we are going through a protracted trial. While normal, dissatisfaction reveals a lack of faith in God. The enemies of God's children must be defeated. In advance, we should resolve to maintain our faith and confidence in God's kindness in all circumstances.

Whatever you are going through, keep your attention on God's promises and what He is doing despite your disappointment or pain. Keep your focus on Jesus Christ, the source and summit of your faith, and He will aid you in developing faith despite suffering.

PRAYER:

DAY 18-BUILD TRUST VIA PRAYER

Bible Scripture: Proverb 3:5-6

"Put your complete trust in the Lord, relying not on your understanding; submit to him in all your endeavors, and he will make your pathways straight."

Although it is a conversation with the Living God, His children frequently ignore prayer. When we pray, we can feel God's heartbeat for the unredeemed, our loved ones, and our spiritual state. We can ask the Holy Spirit to intercede on our behalf when we are at a loss for words.

God has given you everything you desire to progress in prayer. Spend some time in the Lord's presence starting today. At first, it could feel odd, but as you pray and sense His presence, your faith will solidify. As they witness God at work, Christians who incorporate prayer into their daily lives will continue to grow in their faith and trust.

The Christian life is a 24/7 endeavor. We must memorize some information to perform properly; else, we will fall short. We also need to be aware of where to go for the solutions to our problems. We can only accomplish that if we take the time to study the Bible.

It's time to begin memorization of verses if you are having problems trusting others.

Ask your spouse, friends, or even your children to help you memorize a text on trust. Your children could be impressed that you are memorizing the material rather than asking them to do so!

Make a promisc to study the Bible daily and put your faith in the Lord.

Prayer:

DAY 19-BE HIS WITNESS

Bible Scripture: Act 1:8

But once the Holy Spirit has descended upon you, "you will acquire authority, and you shall be my witnesses both in Jerusalem and throughout Judea and Samaria, and even to the ends of the globe."

Many people find it intimidating to share their faith in Christ with others, often because they feel unprepared or unsure how to phrase their conversation.

Pray and offer yourself to God so He might use you to share His love with others. Confess your worries and enlist the Lord's assistance in spreading the Gospel of Jesus Christ. You will have opportunities to witness because God will open doors. You'll discover that God is dependable in giving you the words to speak, and the power of the Holy Spirit will impact people's hearts through you. As you move in the sphere of His love and power, your level of faith will rise.

Remember that your role as a witness is to communicate everything you have experienced rather than to save people; that is God's responsibility! Therefore, as you strive to communicate, do it with a heart of prayer for the people you speak with and that the Holy Spirit will lead your words. To do His work in the hearts of others around you, ask God to operate through you in Word and deed. As yoWordare obediently, pray consistently and rely entirely on the work of the Spirit.

Prayer:

DAY 20-CONTACT THE HOLY SPIRIT

Bible Scripture: John 14:15-17

"If you truly love me, you will obey my instructions. And I'll ask the Father to send you another Counselor who will stay by your side forever. He is the Truth Spirit. The world cannot receive him since it does not see or know him. However, you know him because he is still present in you and will be."

We have all encountered circumstances where we must step out in faith but hesitate. How can we get through the times when fear wins out over faith? Our Heavenly Father gave us everything we require via the power of the Holy Spirit a long time fulfill.

Next time you find yourself in a circumstance that makes you want to back away, pause and pray since Jesus referred to Him as our Helper in John 14:26.

Because we have varied relationships with God and Jesus Christ, the Holy Spirit communicates differently. However, there is one constant among believers. A long-term relationship is a foundation for effective, powerful, healthy communion with the

Holy Spirit. Making a good connection takes time. Time, effort, focus, sincerity, reliability, silence, and constancy.

Speaking with the Holy Spirit is like talking to your truest, most authentic, and wisest self. The best approach to communicate with the Holy Spirit is to be still, give Him room to speak, and then take notes on what you perceive He is saying. Rarely do voices in my head say things like, "Start a newsletter called Echoes of the Spirit and a blog called Echoing Jesus!" Instead, I sense that I need to act, speak, or go somewhere.

Ask the Holy Spirit to strengthen your faith to move on and fulfill what God is calling you to accomplish. Your faith in Him will grow as you fulfill the task, He has given you, and watch Him use you to accomplish wonderful things.

Prayer:

DAY 21-FAST AND PRAY

Bible Scripture: 1 Corinthians 7:5

"Only if both parties agree and, for a limited period, refrain from depriving one another so that you can devote yourself to prayer. Then reunite so that Satan cannot seduce you due to your lack of restraint."

Fasting is another spiritual practice to strengthen our prayer lives, worship, and Bible study. In Matthew 6:5–18, Jesus discussed the benefits of both prayer and fasting. He also served as an example of these practices by fasting in the wilderness before starting his ministry (Luke 4:1-2).

Some translations of Mark 9:29 and Matthew 17:21 also imply that fasting and prayer can help people achieve specific spiritual victories. Jesus retorted, "This sort can come out by nothing but prayer and fasting," when his disciples failed to cast out a demon (Mark 9:29, NKJV).

Scripture also emphasizes the value of fasting and prayer before significant occasions or choices in other chapters. For instance, Esther pleaded with the people of God to fast before she went to King Ahasuerus to stop the genocide he had authorized (Esther 4:16). We also witnessed the church fasting and praying before appointing ministry leaders in Acts 13:2-3 and 14:23.

You will experience a breakthrough and God's presence if you humble yourself before the Lord, repent, and seek his face. Fasting and prayer are challenging, and developing spiritual strength takes time. Think about starting small. Do not lose heart if you are unable to complete your first fast. It's possible that you initially attempted to fast for too long. We undergo positive changes while we fast.

PRAYER:

DAY 22-BE A FAITHFUL STEWARD

Bible Scripture: 1:7-8

"As God's steward, an overseer must be beyond reproach. He must not be conceited, irritable, violent, intoxicated, or eager for riches, but rather hospitable, a lover of goodness, self-controlled, righteous, and disciplined."

Christians frequently yearn for more faith despite their lack of faithfulness in what they already possess. Being obedient to what you already know you ought to do but are not doing is one of the best means to expand your faith.

James 1:22 encourages us to put God's Word into practice. To build strong faith, start by listing what you already know you should be doing. For instance, you should incorporate regular prayer and Bible reading. Your next move, should they not be, would be to schedule time for each of these activities. With each act of obedience you perform, remain true to what you have, and you will advance.

Using what God gives us properly is a part of our duty as stewards. We must use our time, energy, talents, and resources in ways that are important to God. Therefore, we must be concerned with the things that stir God if we wish to be good stewards. It should be abundantly evident from Jesus' example that God cares about people, especially the oppressed, weak, and vulnerable. God has commanded us to participate in his plan to use the Gospel to rescue the world (Matthew 28:16-20).

According to James 1:27, "Pure and flawless belief is this: to attend to orphans and widows in their misery and to avoid oneself from being polluted by the world.

PRAYER:

DAY 23-TAKE DOWN BARRIERS TO PEACE

Bible Scripture: Roman 14:19

"So let's pursue the things that promote peace and those that can help one another grow."

The absence of tranquility makes it difficult to develop faith and confidence in God. We are often unsure of what to do, and the absence of tranquility halts our development. Other times, we may not be certain of God's will, and our lack of peace prevents us from moving on.

God guarantees in Isaiah 26:3 that "Those whose hearts are solid because they trust in you" will be "Kept in perfect peace." The key to finding serenity is to put your trust in God. Ask God for direction and have faith that He won't let you stray even a little from what He has planned for your life. If you believe what He says is true and take Him at His Word, your mind will be dominated by His perfect calm, leading to the growth you want.

PRAYER:

DAY 24-WALK CLOSELY WITH JESUS

Bible Scripture: Romans 13:13

"Let us walk with dignity, as in the daytime: not in revelry and intoxication; immoral sexual behavior and promiscuity; not in contention and resentment."

God commanded us to "Walk in Christ Jesus the Lord" in Colossians 2:6-7. Your faith will receive the roots it needs to grow as you walk closely with Him.

Here are some doable suggestions to help you get closer to the Lord Jesus. Read about Him in God's Word first. You will inevitably move to the next phase as you learn more about what He has done and spoken. Worship Him and thank Him for His love and sacrifice. Then, follow His direction in all aspects of your life, including your devotion to others. You will grow in your faith as you walk with Him.

Your desire to follow God and be his friend will be greatly stoked when the zeal of God seizes your heart. Imagine developing a relationship with God while living a 365-year life like Enoch! One can only imagine the magnificent intimacy levels Enoch uncovered. Perhaps God became sick of withholding himself since Enoch's heart yearned for more of him so fervently. Maybe God was saying in His heart, "You love me with such a pure and lovely desire, Enoch, that I no longer want to say "No." I'll grant your request and reveal my face to you. Up you go!"

PRAYER:

DAY 25-SPOT AREAS OF UNBELIEF

Bible Scripture: Psalms 78:22

"As a consequence of their shortage of faith in God and His atoning power."

A portrayal of what happens when disbelief confronts Jesus Christ is seen in Mark 9:24. The experience with the Lord in this parable highlighted the Father's lack of faith when he placed a serious, individual need before the Lord. Identifying your unbelief before you are in a difficult situation is essential since it weakens your trust.

By saying those words, you are committing to upholding the covenant's provisions and attaching yourselves. And you're suggesting that if either you or he broke the terms of the covenant, "Whoever violates the pact should suffer the same fate as animals, whether me or him. Let us spill our blood as the animal did. Let us lose our lives just like the animals do. Let us pass away tragically, just like the animals do." In those days, a promise was made in this manner.

Request that God see into your heart, then record what He finds. Utilize God's Word to combat your lack of faith. Your faith and confidence in God will grow as you transition from disbelief to belief.

But you can have faith that God alone will accomplish it. God gave His Son Jesus Christ for you, didn't He? And how can God not freely give you everything else if He has freely provided Jesus Christ for you? If you haven't read your Bible or prayed to God today, it's possible that you haven't prayed for the things God wants you to pray for. Even if you have, it's possible that you haven't sought Him out in prayer. Perhaps you missed participating in community life today. You might not have made an effort to recall Jesus throughout meals, whatever that may be. Maybe this is a good opportunity for you to say, "Lord, please help me to grow in my faith. Assist me in standing up for my faith today, to take in the Gospel, and to think of Jesus and His love."

PRAYER:

DAY 26-TRUST GOD WITH YOUR PAIN

Bible Scripture: 1 Corinthians 1:4

"He comforts us in all our pain so that, through the consolation we receive from God, we may be able to solace those who are in any type of affliction."

It is simple to doubt God's goodness when adversity strikes. Then your heart compares God's goodness to your desires, which results in disappointment. When things do not come out as you had hoped, resist believing God does not care about you. No matter what occurs, you must set your heart and thoughts on God's promises and have faith in Him.

God is in charge of determining why you are experiencing hardship. He is prepared to discuss your most pressing needs with you since he is aware of them. Ask Him to give you the necessary spiritual resources since He has already prepared enough faith for you to prevail. Nighttime suffering exists, but with Him, joy comes in the morning.

We construct an unstable picture of God when we judge him in light of our shifting circumstances.

But a single moment does not make up a lifetime. We exist as characters who cannot foresee the conclusion or fully comprehend the plot, living in the middle of a story.

So, despite our limited comprehension, we must keep the author's credibility in mind.

Prayer:

DAY 27-START WORKING

Bible Scripture: James 2:14

"My brothers, what good does it do if someone asserts to have faith but does not act on it? Can faith save him?"

Faith without works is dead, according to the Word of God. This implies that we cannot merely pray and assign God our work. He won't leave His throne to carry out the task He has given YOU the authority and capability to complete.

Have you started the home-searching process if you wish for a new house? Have you been setting up funds for the down payment? Are you looking into the market for houses that suit your means? A budget, do you have one?

Have you revised your resume if you're looking for a more desirable job? Are you looking to further your education to improve your abilities?

By walking by faith, you imply to do something. Making a strategy and executing the necessary effort are prerequisites for walking.

Let us be doers of the Word, not simply headword, as we proceed on this journey of walking by faith.

Prayer:

DAY 28-PRAY FOR STRENGTH

Bible Scripture: Psalm 55:22

"He will not allow the righteous to be shaken, so cast all your worries on Him. Whatever struggles we may face, we can bring them before the Lord, who will give us the courage to overcome them."

Whether psychologically, emotionally, spiritually, or physically, we have all suffered periods when we feel incapable. When the unusual occurs, we are unsure of what to do. Taking a period to pray during these trying times can be a great help. God is ready and willing for us to cry out to Him and seek help.

God commands us to turn to him for rest when we are burdened. We can start to feel the power of prayer when we come to God in humility and sincere faith to ask for physical and spiritual strength. Here, you may find some of the most effective prayers for courage that might serve as an example. You are welcome to modify these prayers to reflect your circumstances and your need for courage. You'll be strong if you put your trust in God.

In contrast to our current instant gratification culture, abiding by God's promises takes time. I do not deny that humans are capable of immediate healing. We can. But we must remember that pursuing these rewards is not the secret.

Entirely these things will be strengthened to you if you seek God first (Matthew 6:33), and "Your roots will grow deep into God's affection and knowledge of His steadfast love for you."

Faith is coupled with trust. We can cling to the assurance that God will provide for us by faith and through faith. He won't ever leave us or let us down. He will provide for our needs at the appropriate time. Faith reassures us that we can trust God and that he will never let us down.

When we are weak, in need, or fearful, we can pray to God and ask Him to give us strength. Regular communication with God during the good times gives us the courage to contact Him during challenging times.

Yes, even when that is the only time we seek Him, God hears and answers our cries of desperation. However, this is much simpler when we share every aspect of our lives with him through prayer.

When we need strength, we can turn to God. This is simple. It entails prayer, faith, and trust. And the more often we do so, the simpler it gets to draw power from God. When we encounter challenges in life, we can turn to God and ask for his assistance. God can give us courage.

Prayer:

DAY 29-PRAY FOR WISDOM

Bible Scripture: Colossians 2:2-3

"To know the enigma of God, namely Christ, in whom all the jewels of wisdom and knowledge are hidden, I want them to be strengthened in Spirit and connected in love. This will enable them to receive the entire riches of perfect insight."

Because only God succeeds in attaining his intended aims without fail, I contend that the highest human intelligence has the greatest chance of success in achieving the intended, righteous goal. God's wisdom always succeeds in reaching his intended purposes because of his broad awareness of reality, situational insight, and essential resolve.

That is not true of finite humans, whether believers or atheists. Because only God can ensure the accomplishment of his wisdom, even the greatest human wisdom—with all its factual knowledge, situational insight, and essential resolve—will occasionally fail to achieve its intended, virtuous purposes.

I mentioned a few minutes ago that I would attempt to define wisdom in the broadest sense first before getting more particular. So, here's my more detailed explanation: The highest human wisdom is the combination of factual understanding, situational awareness, and the required resolve that will enable one to achieve complete and enduring happiness.

You'll also notice that I didn't add a qualifier like "Having the highest chance of success in achieving happiness." Because God has decreed that nothing in the cosmos can prevent his redeemed people from experiencing complete and enduring enjoyment in his presence when they act by the guidance of the Holy Spirit, there is no stopping this wisdom.

We impart a private and hidden wisdom of God [that is, he imparts it to believers], which God decreed before the generations for our glory. That divine wisdom, planned for his people before creation, cannot fail, according to Paul in 1 Corinthians 2:7. We cannot fail to achieve the glory and joy that God predetermined for us before the ages when that wisdom is delivered to us by the Holy Spirit in the new birth. We walk by that wisdom in faith.

Therefore, my more detailed definition of the best human wisdom is factual knowledge, situational insight, and the necessary resolve that together succeed in achieving full and everlasting happiness. This wisdom is the kind we need, the way we can have, as a blood-bought gift of Jesus, by the Spirit, through faith.

Will we remember that "All aspects are yours, Paul or Apollos or Cephas or the nation or life or demise or the existing or the forthcoming — all are yours, and you are Christ's, and Christ is God's" (1 Corinthians 3:21–23) and turn away from the wretched benefits of boasting in men?

So, I implore you to acquire wisdom. "Be a fool so that you may learn wisdom." A smart, upbeat, and joyful fool. For Jesus (1 Corinthians 4:10).

Prayer:

DAY 30-GIVE THANKS ALWAYS

Bible Scripture: Psalm 103:1-4

"My soul, worship the LORD; all the depths of my being, exalt His holy name. Honor the LORD, my Spirit, and never forget His blessings. He is the one who cleanses you from all sin and heals all of your illnesses. He also saves your life from the pit and gives you a crown of love and compassion."

Have there ever been circumstances where you gave someone something of tremendous worth but received little appreciation in return? Although it may not have been extremely valued (in terms of money), it meant a lot to you (perhaps your time away from home). Do you still recall how hurt you felt when your efforts went unappreciated? God is sovereign. However, I can't help but feel that the believer's praise to God should primarily be expressed as gratitude for the countless benefits that God has placed upon us. A simple "Thank you" can accomplish a lot.

Thanksgiving encourages God to bless your life. Solomon made a thousand burned offerings to God in 2 Chronicles 1:6–15 before retiring to bed. He received the divine intervention, a free pass from God, divine overflow - more than he requested, and divine overflowing prosperity — silver turned to stones. You did not ask for wealth, honor, or long life; God said Solomon in verse 11. Solomon received these additional blessings from God.

Thanksgiving brings the majesty of God to earth. When God was given loud praises and thankfulness in 2 Chronicles 5:13–14, His splendor flooded His house, and the priests could not stand. As you give God thanks in the name of Jesus, sickness, disease, grief, and demons cannot stand.

Thanksgiving marks the start of a new era. Start with thanksgiving if you want a new period of miracles, signs, and wonders (Luke 22:19-20).

Thank God for all that He has accomplished and will do. Consider that you typically express gratitude to someone after receiving something from them. You express gratitude when someone gives you a present or a compliment. You give a waiter a tip after they serve your table to say thanks. You would have confidence that the waiter would fulfill your expectations if you gave him a tip before receiving service.

It's a fantastic act of faith when you give God thanks BEFORE you receive what you ask for in prayer! You are announcing that it is finalized and that you are so confident that God will accomplish it that you can give him thanks in advance! In essence, you were given the solution instantly through trust; all left is for it to materialize now!

Are you appreciative of all God has done for you? If so, the Bible offers a variety of ways for us to give God appreciation. We might discover that there are much more things for which we should be grateful than we first thought when we enter eternally.

Have a happy Thanksgiving, and may God bless you!

PRAYER:

CONCLUSION

Although not all-inclusive, these steps are unquestionably a solid place to start. God has gone to tremendous lengths to enable you to establish a personal relationship with Him, and the foundation of that relationship is faith and trust. Let this list serve as your initial effort to please God.

It is unthinkable to please God without faith. However, the Bible records several instances of people who did honor God. The significance is that it is doable, therefore, ask for the necessary faith and do so in prayer. We beg You now, O Lord, for support and resources so we can live honorable and chaste lives. Amen, in the name of Jesus.

PRAYER

I am confident in your goodness, Heavenly Father. The ideal Father imaginable. Your Word declares that your word is true to all of your promises and that you are full of loving kindness toward me. On some level, Lord, I do believe all of this. On a deeper level, however, my misgivings persist. Particularly when I am walking through this valley. Father, I think, "Help me overcome my doubt and give me confidence that you can deliver on all your promises."

Amen, in the name of Jesus.